The Girl Who Loves Her Dress

by Sandra Arauz
Illustrated by Jamie Jamandre

Tellwell Talent
www.tellwell.ca

ISBN
978-0-2288-5811-9 (Hardcover)
978-0-2288-5810-2 (Paperback)

In the morning, Joy
wants to wear her dress

In the evening, Joy wants to wear her dress again.

She feels so mad when she can't find her dress.

She feels so sad
when she can't wear
her dress.

She grabs her
magnifying glass and
begins to search for her
dress all around
her room.

She looks under her bed.

She looks in her closet.

She sits down in her quiet space.

She takes a deep breath in. Then, she breathes out to let her feelings out.

Finally, she goes to the living room.

She is so surprised.

To see her dress
on the couch.

Joy finds her dress.
She kisses her dress.

Joy puts on her dress,
and she feels so,
so happy.

www.ingramcontent.com/pod-product-compliance
Lightning Source LLC
Chambersburg PA
CBHW040938100526
44816CB00002B/35